Love & Re-Marriage
Guided by Christ

JOHN & BARBARA GOSS

The red heart puzzle with light streaming through the cross shaped hole
in the center symbolizes Christ's Guiding Light in the center of our love.

We are all imperfect and broken people, thus all the pieces of the puzzle.
It is our goal to put all our pieces together
and have a healthy, loving relationship guided by Christ.

Give Praise Serve Publishing

www.givepraiseserve.com

Any references to historical events, real people, or real places are used fictitiously. Names, characters, and places are products of the author's imagination.

Front cover image from iStockphoto, © 2009 James Group Studios.

Library of Congress Control Number: 2018906834

Love and Re-Marriage Guided by Christ/John Goss and Barbara Goss–First edition

Give Praise Serve Publishing, an imprint of Manifest Publishing

ISBN: 978-1-944913-42-7

Contents

This book is dedicated to our parents

Robert & Rosa Brinkley

and

Robert & Margaret Goss

who made a profound impact on us

by demonstrating a strong work ethic

and servant leadership

throughout their lives

with little appreciation or recognition.

*"I once heard someone say, 'hind sight is 20-20'.
I strongly believe, had I been exposed to the
knowledge and wisdom shared in this Christ
inspired book, I would not have failed at three
marriages. I thought I knew how to succeed in
marriage. I didn't know, but I thought I knew.*

*If you are on the verge of getting married, read this
book immediately. If you are thinking about
getting a divorce, don't put this book down until
you have read it cover to cover, as I have.*

*John and Barbara are my personal friends and I
have witnessed the love they share. The singer,
Stevie Wonder can see it and feel it.*

*This book will increase the marriage success rate
of those who read this book.*

To God be the Glory, from my lips to God's ears."

~ Les Brown, World's Leading Motivational Speaker

Foreword

John and Barbara, it's been amazing to watch you both grow and to witness God's purpose and plan being fulfilled in your life.

Thanks for always being committed students as you took the journey through being prepared for marriage. Each session you took notes and asked so many great questions, but we could also see the great eagerness in you for applying the marriage principles to your life.

We are so proud of how you both carried yourselves during the dating process, always honoring God and your mentors and keeping God First!

We believe God honored your faithfulness to the commitment you made to Him, and to each other. He has created this platform for you to be a blessing to so many other couples as they enjoy this season in their lives. They will truly experience hope, healing, and the joys of being married again.

To the readers, this book is an excellent resource for you! The authors are transparent and provided many wonderful tools that you can apply to make your marriage last for a lifetime.

May God continue to position you in the Kingdom for a time such as this. The best is yet to come. We are your proud spiritual parents and mentors.

Drs. Wil and Grace Nichols

www.mymarriageuniversity.com

Pastor Wil Nichols is the founder and pastor of Victorious Praise Fellowship Church of God in Christ, a progressive outreach ministry in North Carolina. He is a first-class husband, dedicated father, and a committed shepherd to the Body of Christ.

Dr. Grace Nichols accepted Christ at the age of 13 and was called into the ministry at the age of 16. She is the CEO of Triangle Marriage and Family Life Center and is honored to be married to her wonderful husband. God has blessed them with two beautiful children.

John's Story

Why oh, why, did I make the mistakes that I did in my first marriage? Why was I unfaithful many years ago, early in the marriage? I knew better. Why did I no longer love, honor, and cherish my wife? Why could we not work together preparing or reviewing our budget and paying bills without getting frustrated and aggravated with one another? Why was I no longer excited to get home from work and spend time with her? Why did I stop loving her?

Our marriage suffered from loss of trust, security, and respect. Ultimately, our love for one another dwindled due to serious trust issues.

My ex-wife was trying to forgive me, then the 2008 economic collapse resulted in the loss of my commercial construction and development business, loss of income, bankruptcy, and foreclosure of our dream home of 18 years. Financial ruin, lack of security, and loss of trust and respect eventually brought us to a time when all the love was gone.

When she said, "If I had another man to go to, I would leave you," that was all my pride and ego needed. It was my ticket, my easy way out. Soon afterwards, I asked for a divorce.

Without Christ in the center of our relationship and guiding our marriage, we had no pathway to reconciliation or glue to hold it together.

Throughout our marriage, I strived to be a supportive and loving husband as well as a good father who was involved in our children's lives and activities. We agreed that we wanted her to stay home and raise the children. It was important to both of us that we instill our values into them, instead of those of others. This required sacrifice from both us. With only one income, money was always short, and the budget was always tight.

I supported her with numerous craft hobbies as an outlet for her to relax and enjoy doing something for herself, instead of always administering to the needs of the children.

When I was not working, I rarely did anything just for myself like playing golf or going out with the guys. Instead, I strived to be home and involved with my family. I took each child out for breakfast on their birthday to the place of their choice. This gave me one-on-one time with them that we rarely got otherwise. I enjoyed it and I believe they looked forward to it and enjoyed it as well. Additionally, I tried to support them in their activities such as sports, scouts, dance, drama, music, and other interests.

However, years of good works and good intentions can be destroyed and devalued in minutes when you stop loving your children's mother and ask her for a divorce.

You see, I not only hurt my ex-wife, but, when my grown children learned of my desire for the divorce and that I had confessed to an infidelity early in our marriage, their image of their father was destroyed. I know my son lost admiration and respect for me. My daughters, who previously felt they wanted a husband like their father, realized that this image and dream was destroyed, when they found out I was not the man that they thought I was.

I needed to get down on my knees and ask God for forgiveness. I had to apologize to my ex-wife, my adult children, and my ex-wife's family and ask all of them for forgiveness.

It has been a long and difficult road to regain my adult children's trust and respect. They may have forgiven me, but they can never forget. That is something that I must live with.

I also needed to forgive myself. I had to decide to move on, to change my life, heal my soul, and not ever repeat the same behavior. Forgiving myself was difficult because I had so much guilt.

I wish I could, but I cannot reverse my past mistakes and behavior. What I can do is change myself and be the best man that I can be for the rest of my life. Additionally, I can share my story and encourage others to not make the same mistakes that I have made.

As both my faith and my relationship with the Lord has grown much closer over the last decade, I have developed a credo, a navigation for life that I strive to live by:

Give Thanks to Jesus, Our Savior
Praise the Lord, Family, and Friends
Serve Our God, Family, and Community

The Navigation for Life Credo

When God brought Barbara into my life, I knew that I wanted to keep Christ at the center of this relationship. More than a year before I proposed to Barb, I designed this heart entwined cross necklace and gave it to her with this note to describe the significance and thoughts behind the gift.

Barbie,

I give you this heart entwined cross, designed for you, to serve as a symbol that I have given my heart to you with Christ first and at the center of our lives. I promise to always love you and I know that Christ will forever be the binding strength and guiding force of our relationship.

With all my love,

John

When Barbara and I got to know one another, we learned that we both had desires to serve God by serving his people to help build stronger marriages and prevent divorces through speaking engagements and conducting seminars. We felt God brought us together and had plans for our marriage to be a light for others. After taking pre-marital classes with Pastor Wil and Dr. Grace Nichols, they asked Barbara and I to prepare a lesson to be taught to couples planning to enter a second marriage. Barbara and I were honored, and it confirmed our belief that our story and marriage could be an example for others. We welcomed this opportunity and challenge.

As we planned our wedding and selected songs, we became reacquainted with *The Prayer*. We love the lyrics of this song: "I pray you'll be our eyes...and...Guide us with your grace".[1] We chose this song as our Prelude to set the tone for our wedding and our marriage.

God forgave me and blessed me with the opportunity to develop a relationship with another lady. Barbara has become my new wife.

We want to give thanks to Jesus Christ, our savior; Praise the Lord, family, and friends. We also want to serve God and our community. We pray that this book will be a guiding force that navigates you through challenges and provides opportunities on the path toward the happiness of a successful second marriage.

PREFACE

Barbara's Story

I am the youngest of thirteen children. My mom and dad expected much from me. They sent me to private school from kindergarten through 12th grade. I always felt the weight of not disappointing my parents because I knew the sacrifice that they made for me to be successful. When I was in school, I was into books and sports. I didn't date a lot in school because I always felt awkward and unattractive. I never got the looks that the pretty girls got in school. I never was asked out to prom. My high school years were not always a happy time for me. Therefore, I did not have a lot of experience with talking to boys and learning the dating game.

Although I was friendly with everyone, I felt alone at times. As I graduated and went into the unknown world, I still longed for attention that I did not receive and wondered, why not me?

Then I was in my twenties and had many dreams of what I wanted my life to be and look like, a young man came into my life and changed my course forever. I met my son's father in a club when I was 23. We dated for a while and I made sure that I went slow. I thought I had asked all the right questions.

This was my first time having an actual boyfriend. After dating for some time, I thought he was the one. We went out on a date one night and ended up at a hotel. He said all the things I wanted to hear and wished that I had heard years before. I thought the night was perfect.

We continued to date until I told him that I was pregnant.

He came over to my parent's house a week after I told him the news. He kept saying, "I cannot believe this!" "How can you let this happen?" "What are YOU going to do?"

I told him, "I do not know."

He came back a week later and asked the same question, "What are you going to do?"

I said, "I am going to keep the baby."

He then said, "You will be raising it by yourself."

I felt panicked and confused, then asked him, "Why?"

He said, "I have a girlfriend and we have two children." He kept saying, "How am I going to explain this? I will deny the baby and you."

My whole world was turned upside down that day and we never spoke again.

I remember telling my mom that I was pregnant. She did not say a word, nor speak to me for a while. Rightfully so. I had shattered her dream of what my life would be.

Dad said, "Well she is an adult and she has graduated."

After the initial shock, my parents rallied behind me and were the best example for my son to live by.

From that day in my life, I decided that I will NOT depend on a man for anything. I decided that I will not wait on anyone, especially a man, to give me permission to do what I want to do.

I created this persona for myself–I became a person who must be in control. It had to be my way or no way. In the end, that persona provided contributing factors that eventually led to a divorce in my first marriage.

I met my ex-husband at a time when I did not know what I wanted from myself or from a mate. The thought of marriage came about because we were at my mother's house. She saw how well we were getting along, and she yelled and said you should go get married.

I said mom we will do it later and I smiled and shrugged it off. Well a couple of weeks later, my mother passed away and all I could think of was that she wanted to see her baby girl married and taken care of. So, we began to plan the wedding.

I remember when I got married for the first time as if it was yesterday. The day of my wedding, I stood in front of the mirror looking at my reflection and knew I should have waited. I knew I wasn't ready, that I was marrying for the wrong reasons, but everyone was outside waiting, and I could not disappoint them.

My ex-husband met me when I was taking care of my parents, working a full time corporate job, and was a single parent to my young son. He knew my schedule from top to bottom and knew my availability for dating was limited. At the time, I thought it was cute that he was considerate of my time limitations. Sadly, this soon became the issue in our relationship that caused the most stress.

My mom had been sick for much of my adult life and I was always around to take care of her and my father. I was the baby girl and I knew I owed it to my parents to always be there. My life was full of everything and everybody. I completely forget about taking care of myself because I was so involved in giving and taking care of everyone else.

My mom passed away on my son's birthday from heart failure. I remember going into the room where she lay lifeless, stroking her hair for minutes and saying over and over to her, "Do not worry about Daddy. I will take care of him."

I remember that I did not cry. I had to be strong and continue because I had another parent and a son who needed me.

I remember that I sat alone in my mother's room where we sat every night before I went home. I turned on the TV and watched one of mom's favorite shows as if my mom was there.

After mom's death, I turned my attention to my dad, because I had to keep my promise to my mom. Every day I went to Dad to make sure that he was getting along. I know he had to be lonely because my parents were married for over 50 years. My father passed away five years later from a car accident.

After my parents died, the burden of caring for them was relieved and I welcomed the uncertainty of where my life would be going.

In the midst of grieving my parent's death, I was still married but I did not know how to let my husband console me. I had thoughts about whether I wanted to be married, letting my husband be the man, or how to bridge the wall that was between us.

I felt independent. My son was an adult, both parents had passed, and I could finally concentrate on me. I had changed much as these life challenges occurred; so much so that my husband did not recognize the person he had married.

At the beginning of our relationship, he knew a woman who was controlled by her surroundings and he knew her every move. After all the layers were peeled away, he met another Barbara who was adventurous and wanted more out of life. That was the beginning of the end and I asked for the divorce in 2003.

I understand now that in a relationship, you both must make time to grow in the same direction. This is a critical point for every relationship.

After the divorce, I decided that I needed to take time to get to know myself and do things that I have always wanted to do. I worked at a major retail store where I was promoted to a Regional position that required me to move from Georgia to North Carolina. I did not hesitate to shift because I felt that God was transitioning me out of my valley. In Georgia, I felt like I had outgrown myself and I needed to stretch and see what I was capable of. I did not see a plan of exit other than to move.

I always say that God has a sense of humor because of the timing of the promotion. God knew that if either one of my parents was still alive or my son was not an adult, I would not have had the courage to move.

After being in North Carolina for a while, I knew I needed a church home and I found one that gave me the teaching that I was seeking. At that time in my life, I was so hungry for God and the Victorious Praise Church in Durham, NC gave me the connection. I am still a faithful member.

While I was traveling all over North Carolina and Virginia, I made a promise to myself and

God that I would not get heavily involved in any relationship. I knew for me to be in my next relationship, I had to do work on myself. I made sure then (and now) to have motivational books and CDs near me. I remember at the time I was reading *The Value in the Valley* by Iyanla Vanzant[2] and I saw myself and my life in the book. Since my son's father, I allowed myself to be second or third, but never the priority.

I kept my heart and head protected. I dated some throughout the years, but never allowed anyone to get close. When I felt he or I were beginning down that road of seriousness, I would always do something—anything—that would keep the relationship from going anywhere. I remember one time in particular when I was on a date and the guy asked me why I was starting an argument. I said, "I don't know."

I went home that night and thought about his question. It was then I realized that I could not continue to go on this way and drag past hurts into every relationship or situation. I had to change my actions and my thoughts, and trust that the rest would come.

It was a simple question that helped me to open my heart and learn to focus on me! Focus on my desires! Dream again!

The traveling was a bit much and I decided that I did not want to be on the road anymore. Because I was concentrating on me and everything was great, I wanted to be in a relationship. Before anyone could love me, I had to love ALL of me. If I could put myself as a priority, then the person that came into my life could treat me as a priority. I then felt I could be first and deserve it. I was ready to love, be in love, and give all of myself to someone. I was hopeful again.

I felt that it was time. There were still issues. For instance, when I would meet men who would say, "You do not look like you need a man" or "You look like a lot of work." I took offense to those statements. If a woman is single and she takes the time to put herself together for herself, men should have no reason to take offense to that, but some do.

I remember an instance when I was at the mall. I had on jeans, a top, and heels. I was styling it that day with a new hairdo, too. I walked into the shoe store and met eyes with this guy. He was tall, muscled, and handsome. He said hello then walked away. He continued to look at me. (I could see him out of my side view. Ladies you know what I mean!) We passed each other twice in the store, but he never acknowledged me after the initial encounter.

I would see a man, our eyes would meet, but he would walk past me as if I did not exist. This went on for a long time and I started to feel something was wrong with me. I began to doubt I would ever be in a relationship again.

I decided to speak to my Pastor's wife, Dr. Grace Nichols. When I met with my First Lady, I explained that I could not understand why I was having these incidents.

She listened patiently as she always does and said to me, "They do not know your worth."

I sat there stunned because that was NOT what I thought I was going to hear. After the meeting, I sat in my car and cried all the way home. I got home, fell to my knees, and raised my hand to God and said, "If this is where you have me, then I am ok with it."

I soon started my position as Director of Sales at a hotel. The stability gave me a chance to grow my relationship with God and to stop all the noise that was around me which did not allow me to hear from God. I had been at my job for a year when I answered a call from my future husband.

John had a construction job in North Carolina that was bringing him from Georgia. He had called the hotel for two weeks with different questions about the area or the hotel and each time he called I was the one who answered the call. I met him in person two weeks later for the first time when he checked into the hotel.

John came into the hotel one afternoon and overheard us discussing our plans for Christmas. I said that I was not going home because my SUV was giving me trouble. John said that he was going to Georgia and asked if I wanted to go home to Georgia for Christmas, if so, he would be glad to take me.

On that particular day, I felt exceptionally well put together. I had on a dress, four-inch heels, and had just finished a successful meeting with a client. I was on cloud nine.

When John mentioned he would take me, I wasn't impressed at all. My thought was, *I do not know you that well. What would we talk about for 10 hours? Can I trust this man who is a guest in the hotel? Is he a psycho who kills women?* All kinds of thoughts like these went through my mind.

After John left, I said to the ladies, "I can't travel with someone I don't know."

One of the ladies at the front desk said, "Mr. Goss seems to be harmless."

Another lady said, "I think he likes you."

The shock of what they said did not resonate with me because dating was not in my view. However, I decided to go because I really did want to see my family.

Before I went, I had to do some detective work of my own. I watch a lot of CSI shows. I got a strand of hair from his brush, took a picture of his license plate, put them in a zip-lock bag, and gave it to the girls at the front desk. I said, "If I do not come back, you will know what happened to me."

It was Christmas Eve and John was supposed to pick me up at 5:00 pm. But, he didn't get there until 7:00 pm. When he finally got there, I said, "You are late!"

He said, "I'm sorry. I had to resolve some work issues and secure the construction job site for the holiday weekend." He took my luggage out of my SUV and placed it in his SUV. John was a gentleman. He opened my door to let me get into the truck.

My heart was pounding a mile a minute. All I could think of was, *why did I decide to accept his offer for a ride home to Georgia? What are we going to talk about?*"

John smiled and asked, "Are you ready?"

I gave him this half smile and said yes. Boy, was I nervous, but it was too late to back out of the trip.

We hadn't pulled out of the parking lot before I started firing questions at John. I believe I asked him questions non-stop for the first two hours of the trip. To think about it now, I wonder how in the world could he have thought that I was date material after that barrage of questions?

I was nervous as a cat and still asking questions when John almost drove off the road. He did that several times throughout the trip! I began to think I had made a huge mistake. My thoughts went from being nervous to, *This man is going to kill me!* and *Why can't he stay on the road between the lines?*

Later, after we had dated for a while, I asked him why he kept running off the road. He said that he kept looking over and staring at me and could not believe that I was in his truck for a 10-hour round-trip. Little, did I know that John went three hours out of his way to take me home. John came back to pick me up after Christmas and we traveled back to North Carolina. The traveling gave us a chance to talk excessively and discuss how our Christmas visits with family went. We learned a great deal about one another.

About a week later, John asked me out. I told him that I could not go out with any guests staying at the hotel. John's job ended, and he went back to the Atlanta area.

Not long later, John had to return to North Carolina to do follow up work on the airport project. He called and said, "I am back in town for two weeks; I am at a different hotel, so can we go out?"

I said no twice and the third time I said yes. What was a girl to do: it was free food?

I did not want John to pick me up from work, so I asked if we could meet at another location. I was excited to see John, but also nervous. This would be our first time on an actual date. I was thinking, (again) *What are we going to talk about?* There was no reason to be concerned. We met for dinner and we were both giddy and excited to see each other. Conversation was effortless.

John and I saw each other several times while he was in town. While we were dating, I told

John that if he was looking for something quick that I was not the one.

He said he understood and it was nice to get out. Later, John asked for a kiss.

Again, I said no, and I said that if you cannot understand where I am coming from then we can end whatever this is.

He then said, "I apologize. I understand. I will not ask again."

Ladies, he said those five magical words that every woman wants to hear,

"You are worth the wait."

This is the second critical point in a relationship: Do not give up who you are. Your body has value.

After that response, I knew John was the one. John and I dated for three fabulous years. Three years of dating can be an eternity to some. The main point of anyone having a short or long courtship is that you must ask the right questions, and know what you will accept or not accept, and be true to who you are.

We base our relationship on making sure that we appreciate each other, display affection every day, and do not take the other for granted.

We were married March 14, 2015. That was the best day of my life. John showed the world how he felt about me. He chose the songs *The Prayer, At Last,* and *I Do (Cherish You)*[3] to show me and everyone that he was happy to finally have found hope and love in me.

This is the third critical point: God will give you what you need not what you want.

Ladies your husband is supposed to find you. John has been exactly what I have prayed for in a man and a husband.

Visionary Designz Photography (www.visionarydesignz.org)

We sincerely hope that our marriage can be a light to others and that this book can serve to improve marriages and reduce divorces. "Divorce rates in the United States have been slowly increasing since 1970 and today some estimates claim the figure has reached nearly 50%, or half of all marriages."[4]

Divorce is difficult and emotionally painful. It is because we break our commitment to one another–a commitment that was made before God. Additionally, we break each other's hearts. Even worse, we break the hearts of our family and children. One divorce is bad enough. However, many people jump into a second relationship and marriage only to find that they and/or their spouse have become unhappy and that marriage is not working either. This may lead to even more broken commitments, broken hearts, and insecurity among the couple, children, family, and friends. We need to stop this cycle from continuing in our society. We need to reach out to God and allow our Lord Jesus Christ to be the center of our relationships and show us the way.

We have shared our stories with you in hope that our experiences will help you not make the same mistakes that we did. We encourage you to develop and maintain a loving relationship and marriage that is guided by Christ.

CHAPTER ONE

What's the Rush?

YOU JUST HAD A FAILED MARRIAGE that ended in divorce. Before you enter a new relationship, take time to reflect and understand why your first marriage failed. Consider your actions. What did you do or not do, that led to the divorce? Even if you feel that your ex-spouse was the cause of your divorce, it takes two to tangle. None of us are perfect. We all have faults. More than likely, some of your behaviors contributed and need to be improved upon or eliminated before entering another relationship.

None of us are without faults or sin. We are all broken people. Do not expect your new mate to fix you or put your pieces back together and complete you. Instead, we must be patient and pray and ask God to help us correct our brokenness. We need to be whole, and emotionally self-sufficient and healthy before starting another serious relationship. Otherwise, we bring our issues into a new relationship, add stress to the relationship, and do not give it the opportunity to be beautiful, new, and the way we dreamed.

So, wait. Wait on the Lord to bring someone else into your life. Do the work to correct your attitude and behaviors. Be patient and prepare yourself to be ready to have another opportunity for a successful relationship.

John Waller's song, *While I'm Waiting*, the song from the 2008 movie *Fireproof*[5], became an anthem for those waiting on the Lord.

While you are waiting–seek the Lord, have the courage and the discipline to prepare for the next chapter of your life by strengthening, repairing, and improving yourself.

> "Wait for the Lord; be strong and take heart and wait for the Lord." (New International Version, Psalms 27:14)[6]

It will happen in God's time–don't force it. We mess things up when we force it to happen without God. God does not need a hand in His plan for us. Just be patient and receive what God has for you in His time.

Take time for quiet introspection and soul searching.

For example: You might say that your spouse didn't trust you and was always getting angry and yelling at you. If your ex got angry with you or started questioning you about where you were, what you did, or how you spent money, maybe they had a good reason to. Maybe your behavior had led them to become angry or loose trust in you.

Once you begin to see some of the things that you did that contributed to the destruction of the happy marriage, you need to take time to think about how it made your spouse feel and how it would have felt to you, if the roles were reversed.

Waiting and Dating

While waiting and performing self-examination, think about how your attitude, behavior, or actions would feel, if they were directed toward you. Additionally, contemplate how you want to behave instead. Once you see the attitude, behavior, and actions that need to change, you need to pray and do some soul searching to learn where it came from to gain understanding and make corrections. In time, after you believe that you have changed, you may be ready to date someone new. But remember to wait, be patient, and take it slow. Do not try to quickly enter another serious relationship. Make sure that all the broken pieces of your soul have been put back together again.

While you are waiting...

1. Seek the Lord.
2. Don't force it.
3. Take time for quiet introspection.
4. Take time for soul searching.
5. Perform self-examination.

Now, when the Lord provides an opportunity to date someone, go ahead with a new attitude and behavior.

However, you must be genuine, it cannot be phony.

The attitude and desire behind the behavior must be changed and be real. If your new behavior is not real, people will see through it and it will not be accepted. You will be rejected. Therefore, you must take this seriously to do the work to make real and positive change. Be patient, humble, and genuine.

After you have gone through self-examination, changed your attitude, your behavior, and healed your broken soul, enjoy the opportunity to meet new people, enjoy their companionship and build new relationships.

Ladies–please remember one thing:

> *"Any man can treat a lady right for one night, but it takes a real man to treat her right for the rest of her life."*[7]

Be patient, humble, and genuine.

Which one will you choose while you wait on your mate? Waiting patiently for the right person takes courage, it takes self-awareness and self-confidence for any person who is willing to wait on the RIGHT person that God has intended for them.

Dating is the most crucial part of getting to know who you will potentially spend your life with. Dating is not supposed to be rushed. Why is it that we want to put the carriage before the horse? What happened to a woman being a lady and the man being a gentleman?

Courtship is a lost art that we need to recapture to have that deep love that we so deserve. You may not need to date for over three years like we did. However, you do need to be patient and take the necessary time to make sure you truly know your partner and have discussed all the important subjects prior to committing to marriage.

Important Subjects to Discuss (The six F's):

1. **Faith** (What do you believe? How strong is your Faith? Prayer? Read Bible? Church?)

2. **Family** (Past, Present, and Future)

3. **Friends** (How close? Males? Females? Influence–Good or Bad?)

4. **Finances** (Debts, Expenses, Savings, Income, Spending Habits, Budgeting)

5. **Focus** (What is important to you? Priorities?)

6. **Fears** (e.g., marriage commitment, parenting, career, professional license exam)

The waiting and dating process is like a game of chess. It requires patience, selective movement, studying your opponent, learning the behaviors that are not spoken. It also requires not giving all the information out at one time. When John and I were dating, it was very important to get to know each other, what our goals were, and what the goals for the relationship were.

The process of dating and waiting is the element of being raw and vulnerable and letting that person into your most inner self. John and I had both been married before and we were very transparent in telling each other what role we each played in the demise of our first marriages. In John's case, it was actions that caused loss of trust, security, respect, and ultimately love. In Barbara's case, family, employment, life style, and priorities.

If you are not ready to be transparent with yourself and your potential partner, then you are not ready to have someone in your life permanently.

Questions

1. Do you wait on the Lord to guide you or do you push on and force things to happen without the Lord's blessing and mess things up?

2. Have you waited and reflected on your behavior and role in the failure of your first marriage?

3. Have you in the past or are you currently ignoring warning signs?

   Do you still have issues or behaviors that need to be corrected, but have already jumped into another relationship?

4. What will you accept while dating?

   Dishonesty? Disrespect?

   Partner too aggressive sexually?

   Not considering your feelings?

5. How do you tell your potential spouse that their behavior is not what you want or expect, and you are not willing to accept it?

You need to select a time to have a quiet conversation that is free of drama. Simply discuss the facts and if they are unwilling to listen to or accept your expectations, then you need to ask yourself if this is the person that you want to commit the rest of your life to. If they cannot or will not respect your wishes now while dating, how do you expect them to after you are married? However, if they listen and are sincerely interested in your desires and make the changes to meet your expectations, that is fantastic and means a lot.

Also, if they are a great person and you really love them, maybe you need to compromise, meet them halfway, and alter your expectations, so they can meet them.

6. Has the list you created got in the way?

   It didn't in Barbara's case: If Barb had tall, dark, and handsome on her list, she must have lost the list, threw it away, or just ignored it. Because she struck out!

   Strike One—I am only 5' 11"!

   Strike Two—I am not as dark as she is!

   Strike Three—I am certainly not handsome!

"Happy is the
man who finds
a true friend,
and far happier
is he who finds
that true friend
in his wife."

~ Franz Schubert

CHAPTER TWO

First Marriage Mistakes

BEFORE PROCEEDING WITH PLANS to enter a second marriage, it is imperative that we reflect on our first marriage. How and why did the marriage fail? You may be telling everyone and wanting to believe it yourself, that your spouse was the sole cause of the marriage failing and ending in divorce. However, with enough quiet reflection, I am quite sure that you will realize that you, too made mistakes that led to the divorce.

It is important that we admit to the mistakes, pray for forgiveness, and then work on the issue(s) so that it can be eliminated and not be repeated in a second marriage. Going through the pain of the first divorce is bad enough, let's work on realizing and eliminating the mistakes and thereby prevent the pain of a second divorce.

Top 10 Reasons Marriages End in Divorce

1. Lack of Communication
2. Finances
3. Feeling Constrained
4. Trust
5. Expectations of Each Other
6. Meeting Each Other's Needs
7. Lifestyle Change
8. Insecurity
9. Religious and Cultural Differences
10. Abuse

We found this list in an article written by Mary Stearns-Montgomery[8]. The list of reasons is like others that we reviewed. So, let's look at each of these common mistakes and analyze them and make sure that we understand them. Because, we want to be certain that we do not make any of these same mistakes in our second marriage.

Lack of Communication

A couple comes together as one when married. However, if you do not communicate, you will not be able to stay together. Typically, ladies require more words of communication than men. Men need to recognize this and be willing to communicate more to satisfy their wife's need for conversation.

If a man must spend most of his work day constantly talking with other people in person or on the phone, when he gets home he is ready to shut down. He has already used all the words required to meet his social needs.

This can be really amplified when met with a wife who has had much less conversation in her work day, especially if she is at home all day with small children. She is starved for adult conversation and the husband is all talked out.

This situation is going to require compromise. The man is going to converse more than he would prefer, and the wife is going to be respectful of his need for quiet time during the evening. The difference in the number of communication words or conversation needed by men and women is explained in detail in the book, *Men are from Mars and Women are from Venus* written by John Gray, PhD.[9]

In addition to the amount of conversation, there are three different forms of Communication that both partners should understand and practice.

Verbal–spoken words, conversation.

Non-Verbal–that look, facial expressions, body languages, hand gestures, rolling the eyes, shaking your head.

Love–words of affirmation, quality time, receiving gifts, acts of service, physical touch (The communication of love is broken down into five different languages of love by Gary Chapman in the book, *The 5 Love Languages.*[10] 3

Communication is like the circulatory system in the body. Just like the circulatory system is essential to transport the blood throughout the body to sustain life in all the organs, communication delivers all the essential features such as thoughts, information, feelings, emotions, and love that are necessary to maintain a marriage. If the communication is positive, constructive, and loving, the marriage is healthy and successful.

> "Communication is like the circulatory system in the body in that communication delivers all the essential features necessary to maintain a marriage."
>
> ~John Goss

However, if the message, whether verbal or non-verbal, is blocked, impaired, and not delivered well because of a negative attitude or other reasons, then the marriage is impacted. The desired happy marriage becomes unhealthy due to the lack of thoughts, information, feelings, emotions, and love communicated between the couple.

We had to learn to communicate. We met when John came to the area to build restaurants in the RDU airport expansion. A couple of months after we started to date, John completed the projects and left town. From that point on, our entire dating relationship was long distance. If we had not learned to communicate, there would not have been a relationship.

Finances

Finances, or more to the point, the lack of finances, can be an unpleasant subject to discuss and cause a great deal of stress in a relationship. Both spouses must come together and commit to being completely honest about all expenses.

If a spouse makes purchases without first discussing them with the other spouse, it can cause problems. It can be perceived by the other spouse as being selfish and not being a team player. Additionally, it can lead to lack of trust and even resentment.

Also, spouses must be committed to sticking to the budget and financial plan. Unplanned or unbudgeted expenses can wreck the budget and even worse place the couple in financial hardship. Debt and lack of a savings account or fund to fall back on in event of an emergency can cause stress on the marriage.

We have been completely open and honest with one another by sharing all income, expenses, and debts before and after the wedding.

Feeling Constrained

All of us enjoy freedom. Single life provides freedom. However, being single, alone, and free can also bring times of loneliness. Since you are reading this book, you must have the desire to have a companion to love and share your life with. Therefore, you are looking forward to being with someone and sharing your life with them. When a person gets married for the first or second time, there is a tendency to want to keep the singleness mindset. The couple must find common ground with each person having their own time, interests, and activities, and also keep the marriage front and center.

When we are not allowed to do what we want to, we are not only unhappy, but begin to resent and have negative feelings toward a spouse who is involved in restricting us. In time, this can grow to be a major wedge that can split the marriage.

It is important that each spouse have time on their own to pursue their outside interests. Then when you come together you are fulfilled, your individual desires are met, and you are ready and excited to share great and happy times together.

Our relationship has always contained a great deal of out of town work time away from one another. When we come together, we cherish it and enjoy it.

Trust

Trust is huge. If we lose trust in our spouse, it is hard to completely regain it. The choices that we make to have an inappropriate conversation or relationship or make a significant undiscussed purchase may only take minutes, hours, or days. However, the erosion of trust may take weeks, months, or years to repair. Lack of trust can erode communication, hinder financial cooperation, and extinguish some of the passion and sexual feelings. Over time, if the trust is not regained, it can lead to divorce.

That is exactly what happened in my first marriage. When my first wife lost trust, it was never regained. Additionally, it led to insecurity, loss of respect and loss of love.

Expectations from Each Other.

Expectations should be based on facts and statements from one another that are a result of conversation and discussion. Otherwise they are just assumptions. It is not good to assume. Unmet expectations can lead to disappointment.

If the unmet expectations were a result of untrue statements, that can create an even bigger obstacle for the relationship to withstand. In that case the partner will feel like they were misled or lied to and trust can be lost as well.

We have open and honest communication where we share expectations, so that there are no surprises or disappointments.

Meeting Each Other's Needs

Lack of communication is the number one reason[8] for divorce and it is certainly a large factor when it comes to meeting the needs of each spouse.

In addition to verbal communication, there is also communication of love. This communication can be delivered in different ways. Not all people receive love via the same love language or by the same type of communication. When people do not know the best love language to communicate love to their spouse, the message of love does not get received or certainly not received as clearly or thoroughly as intended.

Throughout the dating process, we were transparent, open, and honest with each other. While taking pre-marital classes with Pastor Wil and Dr. Grace Nichols, we were exposed to Dr. Gary Chapman's five love languages.[10] We learned that we each had the same top three love languages. Ever since learning this, we have been intentional about using the most effective love language(s) to communicate our love to one another.

For example, instead of wasting our time and money searching for and buying gifts for one another, we rarely ever give each other a gift. Receiving gifts are just not important to either one of us. Instead, we both feel love from 'Physical Touch' such as holding hands, running a hand across each other's shoulders, a hug, or a simple kiss.

Another love language that successfully resonates with both of us is 'Words of Affirmation.' We both feel loved when the other partner affirms their love by communicating and telling the other how much they are appreciated, loved, or how proud we are of them.

Acts of Service are big with both us also and go a long way in conveying love to each other. Preparing meals, performing household chores, taking care of Barbara's car, maintaining a nice lawn, and helping Barb with directions to appointments are all ways that John can show his love to Barbara. Preparing a nice meal, washing, and folding John's clothes, and helping John send text messages and emails while traveling are ways that Barbara can show her love to John.

Lifestyle Change

Lifestyle changes can be career changes, relocations to another city or state, birth of a child, parent or grown child moving back into home or serious medical problems, to name a few. As a married couple, we need to be patient with each other and any involved extended family members. Life is dynamic–things happen. We need to work together, communicate and compromise so that the impact of the quick change in lifestyle is minimized for everyone involved.

For example, consider what happens when a man gets transferred by his employer to a new town. The wife does not know the area or anyone in the new location. The man needs to focus his attention on her during evenings and weekends to help her learn the area and make the adjustment. Since my employment provided the highest income, we decided that Barbara would relocate to the Charlotte area to join me after the wedding. It was my job to make it an easier transition by helping her understand and navigate the greater Charlotte area.

Insecurity

Insecurity can be a result of job change, job loss, or living paycheck to paycheck with no savings. It can also be a result of inconsistent income because of self-employment or commission sales. Insecurity can lead to fear, unhappiness, loss of respect and the desire to make a change which could lead to divorce.

Instead of feeling helpless and insecure, look at what you can do by being pro-active to bring in extra income or reduce expenses and improve the situation. In my first marriage, I caused insecurity for my wife when I left the employment with large corporations to work with small general contractors and start my own general contracting company with inconsistent income. Her father had worked his entire career with one large corporation and that was what she felt most comfortable with.

Religious and Cultural Differences

To overcome religious and cultural differences, you must not only love one another and have a great respect for one another. But, you must also have a strong faith and a strong commitment to your spouse. It is difficult for a man and woman to come together as one and stay together when there are religious and/or cultural differences. In this situation, it is important to focus on the positive. Focus on your strengths—all those items that you have in common and those traits that you love about one another. It is important to recognize and address your differences. But, we must not dwell on them.

We have never received any opposition as a bi-racial couple. We have been blessed to receive a lot of love, acceptance, and no opposition from our families, church families, or business families. However, when we are out in public, like walking through a restaurant to our seats, we do get some stares and looks. Barb tends to be more of a people person having come from a career in sales and hospitality. She looks at all the people, therefore she notices it more than I do. Myself, I design and build restaurants as a career. So, I tend to be looking around at the building features and finishes and I am usually oblivious to the looks that we receive.

Abuse

There are three basic types of abuse: Verbal, Physical and Sexual.

Abuse by any of these types is a result of a lack of respect for the other spouse. Verbal abuse is sinful, demeaning, and emotionally painful. It also displays a lack of respect. Both physical and sexual abuse are sinful and unlawful. Abuse can not only cause physical harm to the body, but it causes emotional and psychological harm that is difficult to overcome. You can also be arrested and go to jail for these acts. Just because God established the role of the man to be the head of the house hold, God did not give the man the right to abuse his wife physically or sexually. Instead he should protect, nurture, love and cherish her.

"In this same way, husbands ought to love their wives as their own bodies. He who loves his wife loves himself." (NIV, Ephesians 5:28)

We have a friend who was in a marriage where she was a victim of physical abuse. It was painful, difficult, and disturbing to watch a friend incur the physical and emotional pain of physical abuse. The marriage ended with a divorce. After all, how can you continue to love and respect a man who beats you instead of protecting and loving you?

"Then the Lord God made a woman from the rib he had taken out of the man, and he brought her to the man." (NIV, Genesis 2:22)

Questions

1. What mistakes did you make that contributed to the down fall of your first marriage?

2. Have you accepted responsibility and are you willing to change?

3. Have you dealt with your issue(s) and changed so that it will not hurt a second marriage?

"Woman was created from the rib of man. Therefore, man should protect the woman as he would protect his own ribs from blunt trauma. Woman, having come from the rib, her role is to protect the man's heart just as the rib cage protects the heart and other major organs in the chest cavity."

~ John Goss

CHAPTER THREE

It's Not What it Looks Like

WHAT GOD HAS PLANNED for you may not come as you visualized. Stop making a check list of exactly what your mate should be or look like. Be open minded to new possibilities.

We, John and Barbara, are an example of *It's Not What It Looks Like*. When God brought us together, neither one of us was looking for a relationship. We certainly were not looking for someone of another color. God had other ideas.

Both of us were trying to recover from financial hardships because of job loss and the economic collapse in 2008. Dating was not on our minds or in our plans. We were black and white and over seven years apart in age. When we began to communicate and get to know one other, something clicked, and we soon knew that our relationship was going to be special.

This chapter is for those who have gone through a divorce, hope to someday find the right person, and marry again. However, it takes more than hope. Be wise enough to reflect on the first marriage, realize some mistakes were made, admit them, and work on correcting them prior to entering a new relationship.

If you have not entered a new relationship, keep your eyes wide open and ask God to show you the right person. Be patient and obedient. Wait on the Lord to bring that person into your life.

The person that God brings to you may not meet the list of qualities that you had made. Have an open mind and be obedient and give the relationship a chance. For example, if you are a hard charging type 'A' personality, you might think that you want and need to find a spouse who has the same type of personality and drive. However, you may need someone who is more easygoing, who can be a calming influence in your life.

We know couples where the woman is the type 'A' personality with considerable drive to succeed in the corporate executive world. The men are much more laid back and easygoing. They help their wives achieve balance in their lives by helping them relax and unwind from a stressful and demanding corporate work environment during evenings and weekends.

Questions

1. Do you have a preconceived mental list of what he or she should look like?

2. Can you be open-minded to consider someone whose characteristics are different from what is on your list?

3. Do you have previous personal experience of seeing a friend or family member who allowed themselves to enter a relationship with someone who would not have been on their list?

CHAPTER FOUR

Let's Keep it Real

NEITHER BARBARA NOR I were looking to find someone to date. I happened to overhear a conversation between Barbara and some other ladies at the hotel. It sounded like she was not going to be able to make the trip back to Georgia to spend Christmas with her family. Well, I hated to hear that someone was not going to be with family for Christmas. So, I just spoke up and let her know that I was going to Georgia for Christmas and told her she was welcome to ride with me.

Barbara was always very pleasant and helpful during our phone conversations. When I traveled to Raleigh and checked in to the hotel, I discovered she was also welcoming, polite, and cute.

I worked long hours building restaurants in the RDU airport, so I was rarely in the hotel lobby. She barely knew me. Therefore, she was reluctant to accept my offer for a ride. However, she was kind and said thanks for the offer and that she would consider it.

After I left to return to the jobsite, some strong convincing by the other ladies took place. Apparently, they said that I seemed to be a nice guy and that it would probably be safe to ride with me.

Barbara eventually accepted my offer for a ride. Barbara was so nervous when she climbed into my truck for the 5-hour ride. I believe she asked me 64,000 questions about myself during the first two hours of the drive. She asked questions about my family, job, faith, interests, hobbies, dreams, and goals.

One of the questions was–What did I see myself doing in five years? At that point, I think my answer was something like–having a better paying job in the construction industry again and getting out of debt. It certainly wasn't–married to you and being co-authors of a book together.

When she slowed down enough to take a breath, I began to ask some questions about her. Well, during the 5-hour trip and the subsequent return 5-hour return trip a few days later, we learned quite a bit about each other. We realized that we had both struggled with divorce as well as job loss and financial issues, because of the economic collapse in 2008. We also learned that we both had a passion to serve the Lord and his people by doing ministry work.

Later, when Barbara and I first started dating, I remember saying to her, "Let's keep it real." You see, I was still feeling the painful emotional and financial effects of bankruptcy, home foreclosure and a failed first marriage. I did not have the money or desire to play the dating games of pretending to be wealthier or more interesting than the guy that I really was. Pretending to be someone other than who you really are is stressful and can grow to be tiresome. You begin to feel the pressure of being trapped in a lie. God tells us, that if we live in the truth, the truth shall set us free.

"...Then you will know the truth, and the truth will set you free." (NIV, John 8:32)

God is also pleased when he knows that we are walking in the truth.

"I have no greater joy than to hear that my children are walking in the truth." (NIV, 3 John 1:4)

Dating is not real. It is also not the truth. When you are dating, you are on your best behavior, dressed in your best clothes, eating out, going to the theatre, or sporting events and spending more money than normal day-to-day married life and household budgets will likely allow. You are not dealing with everyday situations of managing a budget, paying bills, household chores, wearing worn comfortable clothes, and no make-up. Eventually, if the relationship is going to last, you are each going to learn the truth about one another.

From the beginning, we removed the pressure of dating and 'kept it real'. We both felt that we had to be completely honest about what was in our past. See, we both came from failed marriages and we were both still struggling financially because of the economic collapse. We decided to lay down the good, the bad, and the ugly about who we were individually and what part each of us played in our failed first marriage.

That was important, because we could not hide our faults and baggage. It was a humbling experience to be truthful and admit our shortcomings to this new beautiful person in our life. However, just like the previous scripture verse John 8:32, the truth does set you free.

Consequently, we became intentional about the relationship, and what we did not want to see happen in our growing relationship and marriage. Because of being transparent with each other, our relationship became stronger and it continues to become the relationship we have both desired. We really got to know each other, and we didn't waste a lot of money on expensive dinners and date activities throughout the process.

After we were engaged to be married, we reached out to Pastor Wil and Dr. Grace

Nichols. We wanted Pastor Wil to marry us. They offered pre-marital classes and counseling that we eagerly signed up for. It was a great experience to take their classes. We poured ourselves into the classes, performing all the work that they asked. The extensive research and training material that they have put together was fantastic for us to be exposed to and learn from. The books, 'No More Drama'[11] and 'The Relationship Battleplan'[12], written by Wil and Grace Nichols, helped us see the importance of keeping the drama out of our relationship.

Questions

1. Have you ever had someone pretend to be someone that they were not?

2. How did you feel when you found out?

3. Because of the way it made you feel, will you refrain from pretending with someone else?

"Marriage is not a noun; it's a verb. It isn't something you get. It's something you do. It's the way you love your partner every day."

~ Barbara De Angelis

CHAPTER FIVE

Good Old-Fashioned Courtship Works

IT IS A FACT that every adult male is a man. But, not every man knows how to be a gentleman and take care of and treat the ladies with respect.

Guys, if you want a great lady, then wait on her. Have conversations with her. Ask her questions about her interests, desires, hopes, and dreams. Refrain from just talking about you and striving to impress her. God blessed us with two ears and one mouth. Let's listen twice as much as we talk. Listen to her and get to know her and how she is feeling on the inside. Show her respect.

You want a wonderful lady to have for a life time. Don't try to make her anything less to satisfy your lustful physical desires now. Believe me; she will be worth the wait.

Guys take note:

Any man can treat a lady right for one night, but it takes a real man to treat her right for the rest of her life. [7]

Are you a special man who is willing to treat her like a lady for a lifetime? Or are you only capable of treating her special for one night and then take advantage of her after that?

"But you, man of God, flee from all this, and pursue righteousness, godliness, faith, love, endurance and gentleness." (NIV, 1 Timothy 6:11)

Ladies take note:

It is also a fact, that every adult female is a woman. But, not every woman is a lady.

Women—learn how to be a lady. Let the man lead and show you how much he treasures you. Learn how to expect and accept kindness and respect from your date. Allow him to open a door, pull out a chair, carry a heavy bag, and ask how your day went.

A man does not need to shower a lady with expensive gifts to show his love. Instead, simple acts of kindness and respect will go a long way in demonstrating his love and respect for the lady.

Examples of simple acts of kindness:

- Writing her a love note
- Taking care of her car
- Cooking a meal
- Helping with the dishes

Also, ladies you do not have to and should not tolerate a man who is not willing to work an honest job and earn a legitimate, consistent, and dependable income to help take care of you. Ladies, you do not need to be supporting a player or a hustler.

"But the seed on good soil stands for those with a noble and good heart, who hear the word, retain it, and by persevering produce a crop." (NIV, Luke 8:15)

No sex-be patient; know one another first.

Really get to know one another on the inside—talk and learn each other's interests, likes, dislikes, goals, and concerns. Sex will be more than a physical act of pleasure when you know and love your partner. In addition to the physical act, you will share your love for one another in the most intimate and beautiful way that God designed for man and wife.

Questions

1. Do you really understand what it means to be a gentleman or a lady?

2. Ladies, would you like your partner to be a gentleman?

3. Men, would you like your partner to be a lady?

4. Have you been patient and had a courtship and been able to really get to know your partner?

"The real act of
marriage takes place
in the heart, not in the
ballroom or church or
synagogue. It's a
choice you make—not
just on your wedding
day, but over and over
again—and that choice
is reflected in the way
you treat your
husband or wife."

~ Barbara De Angelis

CHAPTER SIX

Open and Honest

A LACK OF TRUST IS THE number four reason given for divorce, according to Mary Stearns-Montgomery.[8] Hiding speeding tickets or making major purchases without first discussing with your spouse are examples of actions that erode trust.

Even though you may think it a small act, when these actions are added together trust and your relationship are the losers.

I know this first hand, as I was guilty of not telling my first wife that I got a speeding ticket. I did not want to hear her complaining to me that I wasted money on a speeding ticket fine. Also, I purchased a new laptop computer without discussing it with her.

I wanted the new computer and was quite sure that she would not agree with the purchase. So, I made the purchase without discussing it with her first.

Honesty and Transparency

Do not hide things from or be dishonest with your partner. Although the news may not be popular, and the discussion may be uncomfortable, being open and honest will not be nearly as difficult or painful as it will be when your partner discovers that you have been dishonest or withheld the truth from them.

"Better is open rebuke than hidden love." (NIV, Proverbs 27:5)

Also, as stated in Chapter Four, God tells us that if we live in the truth, the truth shall set us free.

"...Then you will know the truth, and the truth will set you free." (NIV, John 8:32)

Do not disrespect your spouse. Be completely truthful and live with a clear conscience.

Although it takes courage to be truthful, it is much less painful than receiving the verbal wrath from a disrespected spouse after they learn that you were not open, honest, and truthful.

"Pray for us. We are sure that we have a clear conscience and desire to live honorably in every way." (NIV, Hebrews 13:18)

The lack of honesty is a slow dissolver of a relationship. Dishonesty will create an atmosphere on both sides and cause a trust issue. As you go forward with your relationship, you do not want to allow dishonesty in any part of your relationship.

Questions

1. Was lack of trust an issue in your first marriage?

2. What items or secrets are you keeping from your present partner?

3. If you have not shared, is it that you do not think the relationship can withstand the truth?

"A strong marriage isn't magically created when you say *I Do*.... It's built on a lifetime of *I dos*: I Do love you, I Do cherish you, and I Do choose you."

~ Unknown

CHAPTER SEVEN

Keep the Noise Down

COUPLES OFTEN PREFER going out with other couples or groups rather than spending time really conversing and getting to know one another. When you are out with a group, often the conversation evolves into stories where people are striving to one up each other with a bigger story. Many times, all you come away learning is which people are the ones who like to talk and boast the most. It is good to have friends and party with friends, but couples also need to spend time together, without anyone else.

Often, couples choose to go out to dinner and attend a movie as date activities. I agree, that is enjoyable and a non-threatening activity. However, we shouldn't do this all the time. While watching a movie, we are sitting there without talking for two hours. We also need to select date activities that allow us to engage in conversation, such as walks in the park or a quiet dinner at home. Money was so tight for us when we met that we couldn't afford to go to movies. Instead, we just enjoyed spending time together at home. Our time together was a walk on a nearby trail, a quiet dinner, some TV, or both of us doing work on our computers while at least in the same room and able to occasionally get a smile, a hug, or even a kiss.

Almost our entire dating relationship was long distance. We talked on the phone every day and saw each other in person when we could. In the beginning, it was every couple of months. By the time we got married three years later, it was every weekend or sometimes every other weekend. We talked a great deal when together, but our major conversations were on the phone in the evenings.

When you spend time alone with your partner, sometimes you need to eliminate all distractions. (e.g., TV, radio, music, surfing the internet.) You need to have quality, uninterrupted, honest and humble conversation and get to know one another. Many people either don't understand or lose sight of this and instead try too hard to impress the other person with how knowledgeable, talented, well read, interesting, or great they are. Those who feel the need to talk and brag a lot are insecure and need to remind themselves of how good they are.

If you find yourself in a relationship with a person like this, get ready for a lot of *Hero stories*, as I like to say. If it becomes too much, we suggest talking about it to let them know that you love them and they do not need to frequently boast about their accomplishments to impress you. However, this is a subject of study that we could write an entire book on. We will move on.

> "Who is wise and understanding among you? Let him show it by his good life, by deeds done in the humility that comes from wisdom." (NIV, James 3:13)

You need to relax, show humility, and simply ask your partner questions, then honestly answer the questions asked by your partner. By doing this, you will learn each other's faith, beliefs, likes and dislikes, interests, hobbies, goals, ambitions, and feelings. This is how you can really get to know someone in a calm, quiet, relaxed, and non-threatening environment without distractions.

Examples of questions to ask:

1. What do you like to do to relax?

2. Do you like sports?

3. Do you like to shop?

4. Do you like sweets?

5. Do you dream of living somewhere else?

6. What do you see yourself doing in five years?

7. Have you ever spent time around children?

8. Do you like being around children?

9. Do you pray often and/or read your Bible?

10. Will you tell me about your family?

11. Do you like to budget and keep track of finances?

Questions

1. Are you and your partner more comfortable in a group setting or do you prefer on one time together?

2. Do you find it difficult to discuss serious subjects with your partner?

3. Are you holding back from discussing important subjects such as faith, children, and finances?

"The greatest thing a man can do for a woman is lead her closer to God than himself."

~ Unknown

CHAPTER EIGHT

Extended Families

WE MUST REMEMBER THAT although we have moved on and either have or are ready to enter a new relationship, other family members have feelings, too. There may be children, brothers, sisters, or parents who were affected by the ending of the first marriage. Just because our love for our spouse changed, it does not mean that any or all extended family member's love for our spouse changed. They may not be ready to accept the second partner.

We need to be patient and willing to talk about it with them. More than anything, we need to be honest and open and show them grace, understanding, and love as they process the changes and get used to the idea of you being with someone new.

In our case, my adult children's emotions were still stinging from the fact that their parents were divorced. They were upset with me for my part in the divorce as well as asking for the divorce. They were not ready to meet any new lady in a relationship with their father. Being patient and giving them the time and grace to meet when they were ready, was very helpful. In time, they and Barbara got to meet and get to know one another. My son and daughters attended our wedding and had a good time. We do not see them often but enjoy the times when we can all get together.

Barbara's family has been loving and welcoming to me from the first time that she introduced me to them. They also came to the wedding and had a great time.

> "Let us then approach the throne of grace with confidence, so that we may receive mercy and find grace to help us in our time of need." (NIV, Hebrews 4:16)

Be humble and God will give you the grace and ability to blend an unexpected and possibly unwanted person into the family, especially when children—young or grown—have not accepted the parent's choice to move on. But He gives us more grace. That is why Scripture says:

> "God opposes the proud but gives grace to the humble." (NIV, James 4:6)

Be humble and patient and wait on the Lord. You will receive grace.

"...the grace of our Lord Jesus Christ be with your spirit, brothers. Amen." (NIV, Galatians 6:18)

As the new partner or spouse, it falls on you to be humble and patient when it comes to meeting the new family. You should not try to, nor in truth can you, replace the ex-spouse. Strive to relax and wait for the new family to accept you.

Children and Blended Families

When you enter a relationship with someone who has children you must get to know the children, especially young children who are still living at home. You can't avoid the issue of raising children. You cannot take the attitude that they are not your children, thus they will not have any effect on you. Whether your partner has full custody or limited custody of the children, they will need to spend time with their children doing homework, taking them to practice, lessons, ball games, doctors, parties. All of this takes time. You can either get involved and feel a part of it or you can feel that it is taking time away from you.

Behavior and discipline of the children can result in issues between you and your new partner or future spouse. Both of you must look at this, talk about it, and make sure that you are each comfortable with the situation and what you are getting involved with.

Of course, this goes both ways. You may have children still at home and be considering entering a new relationship. You need to make sure that your new partner loves and accepts your children also. You and your children come as a package deal. If they want you, they get the children and all the joys and challenges that come along with raising children.

As mentioned in an earlier chapter, dating is not real life or reality. Taking the children on picnics, to movies, ballgames, and the zoo are not real, everyday life. When going out for a fun time, everyone is more apt to be on their best behavior. You need to learn how everyone behaves when you are just spending time around the house, doing chores, homework, helping with meals and laundry, or playing and watching TV.

This needs to be done when the relationship is getting more serious and certainly before any commitments are made. You do not want to find yourself married and living under the same roof and then realize there are issues related to the extended family and deciding to talk about it for the first time. It should have been addressed long before it became an issue in your relationship.

Bottom line, when you enter a relationship, the two of you are not on an island away from everyone else. There will be extended family on both sides. If there are young children involved, the dynamics of the relationship are more complicated and can be difficult. It really depends on the attitudes and behaviors of everyone involved and whether everyone is excited to see the new relationship be successful.

Questions

1. Do you have extended family members who are resisting meeting or developing a relationship with your new partner?

2. If so, how does it make you feel?

3. Can you get beyond frustration and show patience, grace, and understanding?

4. What ideas do you have to help your new partner transition into the new family?

5. If there are children still at home–Has your new partner gotten to know the children? Do the children and the potential new spouse like each other? Is the new partner willing to share you with the children? Do they like the behavior of the children and agree with the methods of discipline?

"The goal in marriage is not to think alike, but to think together."

~ Robert C. Dodds

CHAPTER NINE

Ex-Spouses

WE NEED TO BE UNDERSTANDING and respect the fact that our ex is not going to be quick to want to meet our new partner. We need to show grace and respect to our ex and not flaunt our new relationship all over social media. We still have common family members and friends. It is less than honorable and disrespectful to show-off photos of your new partner.

There should never be any secret communication with an ex-spouse. Except in rare situations, it is best that there be limited communication with ex-spouses. You have a new partner. You need to be completely transparent and keep them informed of any communication with the ex-spouse. Respect your new spouse and do not provide any opportunity for your new spouse to become jealous or skeptical of your communication and relationship with your ex.

I have a friend who talks frequently with his ex-wife and you can tell that his wife doesn't really like it. I decided that I would limit any conversation with my ex-wife and was never going to have a conversation with my ex that I did not tell my wife about and share all the details of the conversation.

When it comes to raising children, the new spouse is not trying to take the place of the children's mother or father. The new spouse is your new partner. They must be patient and earn the respect of the children.

Do not get into a competition with your ex-spouse for the affection of the children. Be real and love the children. They need your love and support much more than they need to be showered with gifts or spoiled on visitation times.

We had a divorced neighbor with two boys. The boy's father rarely had any contact with the boys. However, when he had visitation time he spoiled the boys with gifts and let them get by with any behavior. What kind of role model is this father being? Is he teaching his boys to become responsible fathers one day?

Whether young or adults, your children are hurting enough from the divorce and the unavoidable tension between their parents; they certainly do not need to hear complaints or negative comments regarding the other parent.

God forgives us of all our sins. We need to forgive our ex-spouse of any sins.

"No longer will a man teach his neighbor, or a man his brother, saying, 'Know the Lord,' because they will all know me, from the least of them to the greatest, declares the Lord. For I will forgive their wickedness and will remember their sins no more." (NIV, Jeremiah 31:34)

We need to forgive our ex for anything that they ever did to us and maybe they will forgive us for all our sins and misdeeds. Life is too short to hold grudges.

Learn to not be bitter when our ex moves on. Do not allow yourself to be burdened with hurt, shame, and resentment. As you go forth seeking a new relationship, you must forgive yourself for your contributions to your first failed marriage.

Move on with life in a positive manner, don't dwell on the past. Only take note of the mistakes that both you and your ex-spouse made so that you can strive to not repeat these same mistakes in a future relationship.

Questions

1. Are you communicating with your ex-spouse without your new partner's knowledge?

2. What topics are being discussed that the new partner cannot be aware of?

3. When and how did you introduce the children to the new partner?

4. Are the children comfortable meeting the new partner?

5. Did you ignore the warning signs from the children?

"When there's a breakdown in the relationship, one of the most difficult things to mend is the trust. Love is durable. Love can sustain, but trust is very fragile."

~ Iyanla Vanzant

CHAPTER TEN

Show Me the Money

STABLE FINANCES CAN BRING a sense of security for a marriage. When it comes to a relationship and marriage, a woman wants to know that, as her partner, the man will take care of her.

Developing a budget, paying bills, and trying to stay within your budget is not an enjoyable thing for most. If money is tight, it can be very stressful. Dealing with the stress and trying to agree on how money is spent and saved can be difficult and unenjoyable. In fact, an issue around finances is the number two reason[8] for couples to get divorced.

I (John) agree with this, because it was certainly one of the biggest contributing factors to my divorce.

However, developing a plan to pay off debt, build savings and then reviewing the progress together and seeing positive results can be gratifying and enjoyable. It can give you as a couple, a sense of accomplishment and allow you to start dreaming of and having a positive vision of your wonderful, enjoyable, and secure future together. When you are good stewards of the gift from God, you begin to see that you are going to have freedom from debt, can save for retirement, and increase your family's security. You can also have more income available for discretionary spending to be able to enjoy a beautiful life together and accomplish your goals.

We have found that by paying for stuff with cash and using the envelope system as taught by Dave Ramsey, helps us stick to our budget. When we stick to our budget, we have the money to pay our bills and pay down debt. Reducing debt and seeing progress is a wonderful thing!

> "Each one should use whatever gift he has received to serve others, faithfully administering God's grace in its various forms." (NIV, Peter 4:10)

You are forming a new marriage that needs to be open, honest, and truthful. Therefore, you need to merge separate accounts. Dave Ramsey advocates one joint checking account and eliminating separate accounts.

Another way is to have one shared account for all bills and then each spouse has an account for their personal spending. However, the amount that gets transferred into each of those accounts needs to be discussed and agreed upon in advance by both spouses.

We have chosen to handle it this way and we feel this works well for us. What we like about this is that we have the account for the bills, but then we agree to how much we consistently place in each other's individual account for our own personal spending.

Share all debts and credit issues with your partner and future spouse. Do not withhold any information.

If you have a high debt to credit ratio, then desperate financial times require desperate financial measures. Do not let your pride get in the way of taking the necessary action to eliminate debt, save money, and improve your financial situation.

"She went and told the man of God, and he said, 'Go, sell the oil, and pay your debts. You and your sons can live on what is left.'" (NIV, 2 Kings 4.7)

If a monthly payment to a creditor is more than you can afford, do not be so prideful that you don't call and speak with them about lowering your payment amount for a period. In most cases, they will work with you. They just want to see progress that the debt is being paid.

Men, we are bad about this. I (John) have been bad about this. We let our pride get in the way and do not want to talk about not being able to pay a bill with the creditor or our partner. We ignore dealing with it. Guess what? It doesn't go away. It only gets worse. Because late fees are applied, interest charges are incurred, and the late payments are reported to the credit agencies. Then your credit score goes down and makes it difficult or impossible to make future purchases involving financing or credit. Late payments are slow to be removed from your credit history, as a result they leave you with a low credit score long after the debt or late payments have been satisfied.

Purchases should be discussed.

We suggest that couples consider putting a limit on purchases. Do not make a purchase over $100 without discussing it together and making sure that both partners in this marriage are comfortable with the money being spent.

Barbara and I have found the tools that helped get us on a positive financial path in the material and principles taught by Dave Ramsey in his books and Financial Peace Seminars.[13] Many churches offer the Financial Peace Seminar. We strongly recommend that you check this out or at a minimum, check out Dave Ramsey's books at your local library. If possible, I recommend that you do this prior to your wedding. This will allow you to start off on the right financial path from the beginning.

Questions

1. When should you begin discussing finances with your new partner?

2. Are you striving to get your own financial house in order prior to bringing someone else into your mess?

3. Are you willing to be completely open and transparent regarding your finances with your future spouse?

4. How would it make you feel if you find out that your new spouse has hidden information regarding major financial obligations from you?

"Love is not about
how much you say
I Love You but
how much you
prove it's true."

~ Unknown

CHAPTER ELEVEN

Successful Love

JESUS GAVE US A COMMANDMENT to love one another.

"A new command I give you: Love one another. As I have loved you, so you must love one another." (NIV, John 13:34)

It is not only important that we love one another, but we must successfully get the message across to one another. Communication problems or the lack of effective communication is the number one reason[8] for divorce.

Drs. Wil and Grace Nichols are marriage and relationship experts. In fact, they have been selected by the Church of God in Christ (COGIC), an international organization, to lead the organization's marriage ministry teaching on an international basis. For years Pastor Wil

Nichols has included marriage ministry in his Sunday sermons at VPF. In 2015, soon after we got married, Pastor Wil gave a sermon where he taught about the three different types of love. Let's look at the three types of love using the ancient Greek words for love:

1. Eros (sexual)
2. Philia (brotherly)
3. Agape (like God's love)

Eros love is basically just sex. It is that physical attraction that leads to sex. It is the simplest and most basic form of love. It is the erotic passion and love of beauty. Almost all animals experience it also.

Philia love is like brotherly love. It is on a higher level than Eros because you care about the other person and have respect for them and would sacrifice most anything for them. It is that love for a family member, friend, or community.

Agape love is the highest form of love. It is the love of God for man and man's love for God. It is also referred to as the love for one's children and the love for a spouse.

From Gary Chapman's book, *The 5 Love Languages*,[10] we learn there are multiple ways to communicate or show love to one another. However, not everyone responds the same to each language of love. If there seems to be a wall that is blocking your communication, then you need to explore and learn alternate methods or languages to engage in successful communication of love.

For the communication to be successfully received, it needs to be in the language that is best received by your partner or spouse. You must learn the language that your partner enjoys. Then you must show them love by communicating in that love language.

Let's look again at

"A new command I give you: Love one another. As I have loved you, so you must love one another." (NIV, John 13:34)

Jesus is referring to Agape love in this passage "...Love one another. As I have loved you, so you must love one another." (John 13:34)

The Languages of Love

There are five different languages of love. This basically means there are five different ways to communicate love.

1. Words of Affirmation

2. Quality Time

3. Receiving Gifts

4. Acts of Service

5. Physical Touch

If you choose a language that is not important to your spouse, your message of love could go completely un-received and un-appreciated.

For example, Let's say that you like giving her flowers, candy, and jewelry. Or perhaps your idea of love is to spend quality time talking with her at dinner or converse after the children go to bed. She, on the other hand, feels loved when you take care of the items on her *Honey Do List*, such as mow the yard, replace the flapper in the toilet tank so the water doesn't constantly run in the toilet, and take her car for an oil change and car wash. Your love gifts are not going to mean that much to her and she won't feel much love as a result of receiving the gifts. Also, knowing that her *Honey Do List* for you is growing without items being attended to, she is not going to feel the love.

We are briefly introducing you to this concept of the five languages of love. We strongly recommend that you read *The 5 Love Languages*[10] by Gary Chapman. To further illustrate this concept and the importance of knowing your spouse's love language, I must share a share a story from my past.

I made a huge mistake early in my first marriage. During the first couple of months, my first wife would often say *I love you* to me. Believe it, or not, I told her to quit saying that all the time. And I continued by saying, if you say it all the time, it doesn't mean anything. Well, she listened to me, honored my request, and did just what I asked. Looking back now, I don't remember her saying it very often during the rest of our 32-year marriage. Oh, if I had only known then what I know now.

You see, I was young and dumb when it came to relationships, especially with a lady. I was from a family of all boys. Although my parents, brothers, and I were close and cared greatly for one another, we did not show affection. We did not hug, and we certainly did not utter those three little words, *I love you.*

My wife had chosen to use *Words of Affirmation* as her love language to communicate with me by letting me know that she appreciated me and telling me that she loved me. However, I was young, immature, and not very sophisticated in my knowledge of communicating love. I was stuck in Eros love and my favorite language to receive and communicate love was by *Physical Touch.*

By telling her to stop saying *I love you* to me, I caused a major blockage in the artery of our communication of love. She wanted to communicate her love to me, but, I stopped her. Just think of how much more loved and appreciated she would have felt if I had been more mature and aware; had been able to receive her *I love you* messages and then been able to return the communication to her properly and successfully.

Now, looking back at the situation, I can see that I rejected her communication of love.

Which, I would imagine led to her feeling rejected and unappreciated herself. Without us having the knowledge of other languages to communicate our love, our marriage suffered. It was not healthy. There was a blockage and the love messages were not getting circulated completely and successfully from one of us to the other.

Much later in our marriage she read the *The 5 Love Languages*[10] by Gary Chapman. She tried to get me to read it and put it to work in our marriage.

I read the book. However, my heart was hardened after years of a marriage lacking love. I did not have Christ in my daily life.

We certainly did not have Christ at the center of our relationship and guiding our marriage. Therefore, we did not know about or follow the teachings of Jesus Christ.

> "A new command I give you: Love one another. As I have loved you, so you must love one another." (NIV, John 13:34)

The following chart shows the three types of love and the five languages of love. As you can see all five languages of love can be used in Philia and Agape love. However, Eros love is all about physical touch.

Three Types of Love and the Five Languages

Eros	Philia	Agape	Love Languages
	X	X	Words of Affirmation
	X	X	Quality Time
	X	X	Receiving Gifts
	X	X	Acts of Service
X	X	X	Physical Touch

Questions

1. How do you communicate love to your partner?

2. Are you able to communicate love to your partner?

3. Is your partner receiving your communications of love?

4. Are the two of you connecting?

"Let the wife make
the husband glad to
come home and let
him make her sorry to
see him leave."

~ Martin Luther

CHAPTER TWELVE

I Do, Cherish You
(John's Story)

THERE IS A SONG TITLED, *I Do (Cherish You)* written by Keith Stegall and Dan Hill. It was recorded by Mark Wills, and first released in 1998.[2] I loved this song. I shared it with Barbara. The more she listened to it, the more she fell in love with the lyrics. Both Barbara and I can identify closely with the lyrics. The words mean much to each of us. Barb chose the song for our wedding. She came down the stairs and across the room to me while Marshetta Parker sang the song beautifully.

I must admit that originally, because I thought the lyrics were so fitting, I had dreams of singing this song to Barb while she walked to me. I thought that would be so cool. However, after practicing and practicing while singing along with the Mark Wills recording of this song hundreds of times in my truck, I finally realized that I did not want to ruin our wedding for Barbara and drive all our guests out of the room with my horrible singing. So, I gave up the dream of singing *I Do (Cherish You)* and instead just cherished the moment while watching my beautiful bride enter the room and walk to me.

You may have found someone who you are attracted to. You love them, and it is special that they love you, too. That is awesome! You have decided that you want to marry this person and spend the rest of your lives together. This special person is valuable and anything of value is worth protecting and taking care of. You should treasure and cherish your spouse. Just as we praise and honor our Lord, we should praise and honor our spouse throughout our marriage.

"My mouth shall be filled with praise, And with thy honor all the day." (NIV, Psalm 71:8)

Do not take your spouse for granted! Keep the relationship fun and fresh. Have date nights but don't get in the rut of having dinner and a movie for almost every date. Keep spontaneity in the relationship. Do your part to bring laughter to the relationship. Surprise your spouse with new and different experiences.

Invest in the relationship. Take the time and make the effort to make it work.

Let's reflect, for just a minute. In the beginning, I also loved my wife in my first marriage. What happened? Did the flames of passion go out?

We were high school sweethearts who dated for three years in high school and three years of college. Then we were married for 32 years before getting a divorce. We were in a relationship of some kind for 38 years. I have already told the story about telling her not to say I love you to me so often.

Looking back, I see clearly that I poured myself into my career and our children and did very little to strengthen our marriage. We moved from Ohio to Georgia for my career. I was not near family, did not attend church and/or men's small groups to have positive role models that spoke of good marriages and working to make sure that their marriages stayed healthy and happy. Instead, many of the people with whom I worked and associated had been divorced at least once. This is certainly no excuse, but it contributed to the fact that I did little to strengthen our relationship or fight to save our marriage.

I can now see what I didn't do to keep our marriage strong, healthy, happy, and full of love. I held back info about a couple speeding tickets, and a laptop computer purchase because I didn't want to hear it from her. Making those choices disrespected her and caused her to lose trust and respect in me. Years later, when I admitted to having had an affair, she really lost trust and respect for me. I also didn't do the little things like telling her she looked beautiful, telling her *I love you*, or just letting her know how much I appreciated her.

Make sure that you feed the fire in your relationship. Cherish your spouse and give all of yourself to this relationship. Be completely open and honest. Give love, honor, appreciation, and protection. Make the investment of time, share your thoughts. Take every opportunity and effort to absolutely treasure and cherish your new spouse like no other person on the planet.

Make it your plan to go beyond what is necessary to maintain the relationship in the new marriage. Invest in your future together by taking your relationship to a whole new level of love, respect, trust, and passion.

We have a white board in our kitchen. Every week, John expresses his love for me by writing a new loving message on the board.

After doing this every week for more than a year, I (John) still really enjoy writing a new and different loving message to Barbara each week. I also enjoy seeing her reaction to reading the message. The white board is placed on the wall, so she sees it as she comes into the kitchen from the garage.

It is just one simple way for me to consistently affirm my love for Barbara. We both enjoy it.

Here are a few of my messages that Barb has chosen to share with you.

Barbie,

Thanks for being my best friend, best road trip warrior, my lover, co-author, ministry partner, friend to share laughs, prayer partner, and wife.

I love you,

John

Barbie,

It was 3 years ago today, that I asked you to marry me. I love you even more now, than I did then.

I enjoy finding new and better ways, that I can serve you and show my love for you.

You are beautiful and loved very much.

John

Happy anniversary Barbara Goss,

Two years ago, you took my name.

Married life with you is getting better and better.

I am so excited about our future.

I love you, Barbie!

John

Barb,

I enjoy when we share our excitement and blessings with each other. It is all God. He deserves all the glory and praise.

As you said last night, let's remain humble, no matter where this Opportunity takes us. Let's do our part to be prepared to make the most of any opportunity to Serve God.

I love you,

John

Questions

1. Do you absolutely cherish your partner?

2. Are your actions showing your spouse that they are cherished?

3. What are you doing to keep the relationship exciting and fresh?

CHAPTER THIRTEEN

Completing the Puzzle

WHEN YOU LOOK at the red heart on the cover, what do you see? If you had not noticed, the red heart is a puzzle. The puzzle is made up of many pieces. The puzzle represents brokenness. We are all broken people. None of us are perfect and without sin.

Below is a partial list of areas where we could be broken and failing to bring these pieces to the puzzle that represents our relationship.

- Communication and Listening Skills

- Open and Honesty

- Finances

- Relationship with Extended Family

- Relationship with Ex-Spouse

- Spending Quality Time

- Successful Love

- Cherishing Your Spouse

Women, we may come into the relationship broken from past relationships or come from a home where we did not have a father to show what a father's and husband's love should look like. Instead, we go out to find it elsewhere.

Or, we come from a home where the mother was not a mother and you had to be the mother in the household and grow up faster than expected. You lost your childhood and had to try to be an adult when you were still a child yourself.

If you allow God into your life, ask for his help, wait on the Lord, and then do what is asked of you—God can fix your brokenness.

WE can fix anything, but we must have Christ in the center, guiding our every thought, and every move. The symbol of the cross is here to direct, nurture, lead, and instruct us on how to mend our broken qualities.

Our life is like a puzzle.

Our qualities such as personality, communication skills, thoughtfulness, and honesty are the pieces of the puzzle. We must put all the pieces together in the correct place to complete the puzzle and keep order in our life and do our part to enter into and maintain a healthy successful loving relationship. Only

Christ can take us from standing in a valley of brokenness and guide us to come out on top.

"But rebels and sinners will both be broken, and those who forsake the Lord will perish."
(NIV, Isaiah 1:28)

Men, we can come into relationships broken as well. We may not have had a father who showed us how to be the head of the household and truly love, respect, and provide for a lady. Men, we may also *become* broken (e.g., take our spouse for granted, fail to be open and honest, fall short of their need for communication and quality time) and just don't bring all our best qualities (puzzle pieces) to the relationship.

Brokenness comes in many facets. We can be broken before entering a relationship or we can become broken during a relationship. The most important thing is that we realize and admit to our imperfections. Then pray and ask God to help us fix our issues so that we can bring our best self to a current relationship or one that we desire to have in the future.

The goal is to recognize, acknowledge, and work on improving areas in which we are broken and bring high quality, whole pieces of the puzzle so that we can complete the puzzle with the guidance of Christ and have a beautiful loving relationship with our spouse.

Questions

1. In what areas are you broken?

2. In what areas are your spouse or partner broken?

3. Do you and your spouse or partner agree on the areas of imperfections or brokenness?

4. Are you striving to repair your brokenness?

ABOUT THE AUTHORS

Authors: John and Barbara Goss

John is a facilities and construction management professional, who was previously married for 32 years and has one adult son and three adult daughters. Barbara is an entrepreneur/sales executive and was previously married for three years and has one adult son.

Before Barbara and I met, we each knew that if we ever had someone else come into our lives, we wanted Christ to be at the center of the relationship. When God brought us together—

yes, we firmly believe that our Lord God brought us together. We knew that we wanted Christ to be the binding strength and guiding force in our marriage. We even thought that it might be possible for our marriage to be an example and a shining light for other couples that have gone through divorce and desire to have a successful second marriage. After going through pre-marital classes with Pastor Wil and Dr. Grace Nichols, they asked us to consider teaching a class for couples planning to re-marry. We began to outline topics for discussion, research material and draw from our own experiences.

The result is this book, 'Love & Re-Marriage–Guided by Christ'.

We sincerely hope that this book can be a blessing to help you, a family member or friend. We give God all the Glory.

"From being a pastor who has ministered to couples for over 30 years, I find John and Barbara's book to be a great resource for singles getting into a relationship, young couples considering marriage, and those considering a relationship after divorce.

They provoke you to ask questions that you probably would not think of on your own but will really help you prepare for a long-term relationship."

~ Pastor Sam Benton

To contact the authors regarding e-conferences, scheduling in person conferences, seminars and classes or ordering workbooks and other instructional materials, please see the contact info below:

JGoss@GivePraiseServe.com

Barbara@GivePraiseServe.com

www.GivePraiseServe.com

Acknowledgements

Barbara and John would like to give a sincere thank you to the following people for their inspiration, professionalism, wisdom, guidance and encouragement in leading us to the completion of this book.

Drs. Wil & Grace Nichols, Victorious Praise Fellowship and MyMarriageUniversity.com

Les Brown, Worlds Leading Motivational Speaker

Delilah Cordova, Omni Presence Studios

Candy Zulkosky (CaZ), The Writer Success Coach)

Notes

1   Celine Dion, Andrea Bocelli. "The Prayer." By Carole Bayer Sager, Alberto Testa, Tony Renis David Foster. n.d.

2   Vanzant, Iyanla. The Value in the Valley: A Black Woman's Guide Through Life's Dilemmas. 1996.

3   Wills, Mark. "I Do (Cherish You)." By Dan Hill Keith Stegall. 1998.

4   www.Divorce.com, "Divorce Rate", 2013

5   Waller, John. "While I'm Waiting." By Movie: Fireproof. 2008

6 Bible, New International Version (NIV).

7   Anonymous. www.pinterest.com/quoted_thoughts, Quotes and Thoughts

8   Stearns-Montgomery, Mary. "The Top 10 Reasons Marriages End in Divorce." 26 June 2013. www.stearns-law.com/blog/divorce.

9   Gray, John. "Men Are from Mars, Women Are from Venus: The Classic Guide to Understanding the Opposite Sex." ©2012.

10 Chapman, Gary. The 5 Love Languages: The Secret to Love that Lasts. © 2014.

11 Wil Nichols, Grace Nichols. "No More Drama! Relationships." ©2009.

12 Wil Nichols, Grace Nichols. "The Relationship Battle Plan." ©2012.

13 www.daveramsey.com/classes, Financial Peace University

CPSIA information can be obtained
at www.ICGtesting.com
Printed in the USA
LVHW04s0248130918
590014LV00017B/1502/P